CREATIVE
INVESTIGATIONS
IN EARLY ART

Angela Eckhoff, PhD

Gryphon House
www.gryphonhouse.com

Published by Gryphon House, Inc.
P. O. Box 10, Lewisville, NC 27023
800.638.0928; fax 877.638.7576

Visit us on the web at www.gryphonhouse.com.

Library of Congress Cataloging-in-Publication Data

The Cataloging-in-Publication Data is registered with the Library of Congress for ISBN 978-0-87659-806-1.

Bulk Purchase

Gryphon House books are available for special premiums and sales promotions as well as for fund-raising use. Special editions or book excerpts also can be created to specifications. For details, call 800.638.0928.

Disclaimer

Gryphon House, Inc., cannot be held responsible for damage, mishap, or injury incurred during the use of or because of activities in this book. Appropriate and reasonable caution and adult supervision of children involved in activities and corresponding to the age and capability of each child involved are recommended at all times. Do not leave children unattended at any time. Observe safety and caution at all times.

Contents

Introduction

Ms. Lara is introducing her class to an integrated science and visual-arts project that she describes as a moving painting, in which her students will experiment with color dyes and substances that will resist absorbing the color dyes. For this project, Ms. Lara has placed a variety of colored water in small containers. She has gathered pipettes, large tubs, and small containers of cooking oil and liquid soap to be used as a resist. As a resist, the cooking oil and liquid soap won't take on or absorb any of the color dyes the children add to the painting. Ms. Lara invites two children at a time to work alongside her as they explore and create with the materials. As Ms. Lara carefully describes the materials available for the experience, she emphasizes that the children take their time so that they can closely observe what happens each time they add a new color or substance.

One child, Matt, begins by slowly adding drops of color to his tray. While he works, Ms. Lara asks questions such as "What happened when you added the red to the yellow?" and "Ooh, what color will that make when you add it?" Following his use of the droppers full of color, Matt adds a few drops of oil, and Ms. Lara says, "The oil is resisting that color; it's not taking it on." Matt points out the areas that resist and states that they look like clear circles. Matt adds more colored liquid, faster than before, by pouring out the colored water in the small cups that Ms. Lara has made available. As he pours, he moves the cup around the tray, noting how quickly the colors are mixing together. Ms. Lara continues to support Matt's observations by asking questions and pointing out reactions as they work alongside each other.

Reflection

Ms. Lara and Matt worked alongside each other, which afforded many opportunities to talk about the transformations they were seeing after each new addition to the trays. This type of open-ended experience allows for much discussion and provides many opportunities for informal observations of children's interests and understanding. Each child's experience is going to be different based on the materials he chooses to use and the order in which he uses them. An open exploration captures students' interests and gets them excited about what they will experience next. The inquiry-process skills used in this experience provide opportunities for students to make observations, explore, question, make predictions, and conduct simple science investigations.

The visual and performing arts are powerful curricular companions to early science, technology, engineering, and mathematics experiences. It is important for all early childhood educators to create an environment where the arts are a consistent and valued component of the daily life of the classroom, a classroom where the arts are embedded in the experiences of all children and teachers. Embedded arts experiences move beyond the additive approach of an arts-integration model to a more holistic view that values arts experiences that are rooted across the curriculum in meaningful ways. This holistic approach allows teachers and children to experience the visual and performing arts in a deep, meaningful way. The arts serve as a way for children to experience and express wonder, imagination, communication, and thinking. When the arts are integrated into STEM experiences, we can promote children's abilities to communicate their knowledge and understanding through dance, song, drawing, painting, or sculpture. Guidance in this section comes from the National Art Education Association (NAEA), the Early Childhood Issues Group of the National Art Education Association (called Early Childhood Art Educators, or ECAE), and the National Core Arts Standards from the National Coalition for the Core Arts Standards (NCCAS).

This book is designed to provide early childhood educators with pedagogical practices, arts content knowledge, and lesson ideas that scaffold young children's experiences with integrated visual and performing arts–rich STEM learning. You will find information on contemporary creativity and inquiry-based pedagogical practices that you can use to implement arts-rich learning experiences for young children. This book will broaden your understanding of the relationship among STEM content, learning environments, and supportive pedagogical practices in early childhood classrooms. When visual and performing arts experiences build on student interests and understanding and connect to STEM content learning, young children are able to experience meaningful, relevant connections between content areas. This book stresses the importance of encouraging minds-on learning experiences in the early childhood classroom through guided and independent investigations where every child is actively involved. Early childhood educators have important roles in early arts-rich STEM experiences and will act as both guides and facilitators throughout the planning, implementation, and assessment of the creative, inquiry-based experiences presented throughout this book. For young children, arts-rich STEM experiences involve using tools and a variety of arts media and materials, being creative and inventive, developing questions based on observations and firsthand experiences, exploring meaningful content, and sharing their understanding with others.

Creative Investigations in Early Art will support your development of creative experiences in the classroom by helping you to do the following:

- Understand the links among the science, technology, engineering, arts, and mathematics disciplines

- Plan cooperative arts-based STEM lessons that will engage all children in your classroom as individuals or when working in small or whole groups

- Implement classroom experiences that support children's engagement in integrated, arts-rich learning experiences on an everyday basis

- Recognize the power of the visual and performing arts to support children's abilities to discover, invent, explore, question, and communicate their understanding of the world

- Document children's knowledge development with authentic work samples and classroom artifacts

Playful Learning

Play is an essential part of explorations of learning in early childhood. Through play, young children learn about themselves, their environment, people, and the world around them. Playful learning encourages children to explore and experiment in situations where they feel comfortable taking risks and delving into the unknown. Children's play in the early childhood classroom can take on many different forms and functions. When children explore, experiment, and cooperate through play, they learn about how the world works. Children need teachers who are supportive of their play and who work to carefully identify play situations where teacher guidance or involvement is welcome and needed.

Young children bring their knowledge and understanding into their play to further experiment and clarify their knowledge. This process is child driven; the role of the adult is one of supporter, guide, and facilitator. The adult meets each child at his own stage of understanding with intentional pedagogical practices that promote questioning and exploration. Teachers can create early childhood classrooms that honor the ways in which children learn and explore by ensuring that young children have ample opportunities for playful learning and exploration. In the role of supporter, guide, and facilitator, the teacher carefully observes children's play and helps to scaffold their thinking through questioning and providing additional supportive materials and opportunities for guided learning. The visual and performing arts encourage positive dispositions for play in the classroom because of the emphasis on discovery and invention as children explore and manipulate a wide variety of arts media.

Guided Explorations in Early Arts-Rich STEM Experiences

To develop a comprehensive approach, it is important to understand and apply the pedagogical practices that best support young children as they work in the visual arts. Supporting young children as they observe art, explore media and techniques, and create their own works of art requires careful attention to the many facets of art making and art viewing. In a guided-exploration approach, a teacher works alongside students during visual-arts experiences to support observation and listening skills, to encourage artistic expression, and to consider the aesthetic qualities in art (Bresler, 1993). A guided-exploration approach encourages young learners to engage deeply during arts-rich experiences, which helps to encourage creative, artistic, and aesthetic thinking.

Guided Exploration Orientation to Classroom Arts Practices

In the guided-exploration orientation, the teacher's responsibilities include helping children learn to observe, listen, and communicate their sensitivities through artistic expression and to consider the aesthetic qualities in art.

The guided-exploration orientation involves intensive teaching on the part of the teacher, including providing students with personally meaningful feedback on their work and encouragement to continue to build their understanding.

Student engagement in arts experiences includes effort, concentration, awareness, and thought.

Bresler, Liora. 1993. "Three Orientations to Arts in the Primary Grades: Implications for Curriculum Reform." *Arts Education Policy Review* 94(6): 29–34.

As you plan lessons that integrate the arts, engineering, and technology, consider this guidance from the Early Childhood Arts Educator's Issues Group from the National Art Education Association about the types and qualities of supportive arts experiences in early childhood.

National Art Education Association. n.d. *Art: Essential for Early Learning*. Position paper. Alexandria, VA: National Art Education Association. https://www.arteducators.org/community/articles/67-early-childhood-art-educators-ecae

Quality Arts Education Guidelines

A quality early arts education requires that children have the following:

- Access to an organized, materials-rich environment that invites discovery, interaction, sensory and kinesthetic exploration, wonder, inquiry, and imagination

- Access to a wide variety of art media that support two- and three-dimensional (2-D and 3-D) expression

- Plenty of unhurried time, both structured and unstructured, to explore the sensory/kinesthetic properties of materials and to develop skills and concepts in re-presenting their experiences

- A responsive educator who values young children's diverse abilities, interests, questions, ideas, and cultural experiences, including popular culture

- A responsive educator who can support appropriate development of skills and use and care of materials

- A responsive educator who understands and supports the unique ways that young children represent their thoughts, feelings, and perceptions through actual, virtual, and experimental media and processes

- A responsive educator who supports the multiple ways that young children create meaning through conversation, storytelling, sensory-kinesthetic exploration, play, dramatics, song, and art making

- A responsive educator who carefully observes, listens to, and reflects on children's learning, using multiple forms of documentation and assessment

Building Creative Arts–Rich STEM Experiences in the Classroom

Early childhood educators have essential roles in the development of children's creative-thinking skills because these educators can either

Creative Investigations in Early Art

create supportive classroom environments or create classrooms in which children's creative skills are stifled. To incorporate creative learning experiences in the classroom, teachers must design lessons that include opportunities for critical thinking and reflection, while also maintaining a focus on student interest. In addition, teachers must recognize that creativity is a learning process that encourages social interaction and promotes individual ownership of ideas. In the classroom, creativity is a part of the learning process based on children's interests, involves reflection and interaction with other children and adults, and requires children to document and report on their thinking and experiences. When young children are provided opportunities to personally engage with challenging, reflective learning experiences, they are building critical- and creative-thinking skills.

The lesson ideas and classroom vignettes shared throughout this book incorporate opportunities to build children's understanding of the visual and performing arts, science, technology, engineering, and mathematics while also promoting children's creative-thinking skills. Each lesson includes critical elements of inquiry and creative thinking—open-ended tasks, opportunities for social interaction, and opportunities for reflection and elaboration.

Open-ended tasks provide young learners with opportunities to experiment with new ideas and engage in inquiry. Because open-ended tasks promote idea experimentation, they encourage children to focus on the processes of learning rather than on the need to arrive at a single correct answer. Gaining experience with idea experimentation will help support children's acceptance of ambiguity and willingness to make mistakes, allowing them to gain confidence in their problem-solving abilities.

Likewise, providing opportunities for small-group work and social interaction is a crucial component of creative thinking. Working in pairs or small groups will help to promote brainstorming and allow children to learn from and with each other. Such tasks will also support children's experiences with reflection and idea elaboration. These skills are important cognitive tools that allow children to learn from their own experiences and examine their own learning processes. Employing these components of creativity in the classroom will help to create a rich, engaging learning environment for all students.

Recommended Practices and Content Coverage in Early Arts-Rich STEM Experiences

The content of the lessons presented in each chapter of this book is based on the guiding recommendations presented in a position statement from the ECAE and in the National Core Arts Standards from the NCCAS. Both sets of standards are designed for use with young children, and we can use these guidelines to help determine the types of experiences that promote meaningful engagement in the arts for our students. Every lesson presented throughout each chapter of this book is designed to encourage you to explore and implement the types of arts-rich STEM learning that will build children's thinking, exploring, questioning, and documenting skills, in addition to curricular content knowledge. Together, we will explore the types of lessons and approaches to pedagogy that will help your students learn much more than the conceptual facts; we will look for the opportunities that arise during your interactions with students and enable you to support, extend, and encourage their thinking with conversation and questioning in a natural manner.

Every lesson you encounter in this book will ask you to carefully consider your interactions with young children, as well as the classroom environment. The interplay among children, teachers, and the classroom environment is central to the process of learning. The concept of possibility thinking encourages teachers to consider how asking questions, play, supportive classrooms, imagination, innovation, and risk-taking affect the processes of thinking and learning.

The elements of possibility thinking are as follows:

- **Possibility thinking**—a dynamic interplay between children and teachers

- **Posing questions**—questions from children are acknowledged and celebrated by teachers; teachers' questions encourage inquiry

- **Play**—opportunities for extended play periods

- **Immersion**—immersion in a benign environment free from criticism and mockery

- **Innovation**—teachers closely observe innovations in student thinking in order to prompt and encourage

- **Being imaginative**—ample opportunities to meld imagination and curriculum content

- **Self-determination and risk-taking**—deep involvement and risk-taking are encouraged by both children and teachers

Craft, Anna, Linda McConnon, and Alice Matthews. 2012. "Child-Initiated Play and Professional Creativity: Enabling Four-Year-Olds' Possibility Thinking." *Thinking Skills and Creativity* 7(1): 48–61.

Promoting Creative, Arts-Rich Learning in the STEM Disciplines

Classroom components	*Supportive approaches in the early childhood classroom*
Physical environment	• Flexible spaces with movable furnishings that provide space for exploration, display, and storage, and spaces that can accommodate and adapt for small and large groups

Classroom components	Supportive approaches in the early childhood classroom
Role of the teacher	• Provide opportunities for children to document their thinking through drawing, writing, and verbal means • Encourage students to share their thoughts with a large/small group • Ask questions to promote deep thinking and problem solving • Provide materials that can support student inquiry • Closely monitor student thinking and exploration in order to scaffold experiences
Peer-to-peer relationships	• Provide opportunities for children to share their problem-solving experiences • Encourage and support children's use of inquiry-based and creative thinking • Provide opportunities for children to ask questions, design/plan experiments, work in pairs/small groups, test ideas, and document their experiences
Structure of arts-rich STEM experiences	• Provide opportunities for children to connect the arts to STEM content areas, work on problems and projects for extended periods of time, and revisit previous experiences and lessons multiple times to encourage mastery and promote confidence
Parent and community engagement	• Provide opportunities to connect arts-rich STEM experiences to the community and the children's daily lives • Engage families throughout the learning process through regular documentation of children's experiences

Organization of This Book

This book is based on broad categories of early arts-rich explorations: music and movement, dramatic arts, visual arts, and artists and artworks—all integrated into STEM activities.

Each chapter begins with background information on the visual- or performing-arts content presented throughout the chapter. Each chapter also features classroom vignettes to help bring the information on content and pedagogical information to life. Woven throughout the book are arts-rich STEM lessons for young children that are built on pedagogical practices for creative, inquiry-based thinking. You will also find information on recommended children's books related to each chapter's content.

1
Connecting Music and Movement to STEM

Throughout the early childhood years, young children enjoy running, jumping, skipping, leaping, dancing, and singing. They express their excitement and interest through movement. During this time, children are also learning that movement can communicate messages and understanding and can be used to represent actions. Music should also be a regular and consistent part of the lives of young children. Beyond its expressive capacity, music also helps to promote young children's language development and builds fine and gross motor skills during instrument use. The inclusion of music and movement in the classroom promotes experiential learning, in which children build their knowledge and understanding by doing and reflecting on their experiences. There is increasing pressure in early childhood classrooms to have children spend more time sitting and less time in active movement, but it is important to remember that young children learn by experience, using their whole bodies; restricting their opportunities to move will limit their opportunities to engage in experiential learning.

Dance and movement involves children creating mind-body connections. A central idea in movement is *kinesthetic awareness*, which pertains to a child's awareness of bodily sensations and an understanding of bodily movement. Another important concept in movement and dance is *tempo*, which is the pace or speed of movement—the underlying beat of a piece of music can move slowly or quickly, determining the tempo. Rhythm is the patterning or structure of time throughout movement or sound. Locomotor movements refer to movements that allow an individual to travel from one location to another, or in a pathway through space—such as running, walking, skipping, hopping, rolling, marching, galloping, leaping, sliding, crawling, and tiptoeing. Nonlocomotor movements refer to movements during which an individual remains in place—such as twisting, turning, swinging, swaying, spinning, pushing, pulling, bending, opening, and closing.

Musical experiences allow children to experience the expressive intent of an artist, such as the emotions, thoughts, and ideas of a performer. The elements of music include the following:

- **Pitch**—how high or low a note of music is

- **Rhythm**—made up of sounds and silences that are put together to form patterns of sound

- **Harmony**—the sound of two or more notes heard simultaneously

- **Timbre**—the tone quality that distinguishes one source of sound from another

- **Form**—the overall organization of a piece of music (patterns)

- **Dynamics**—the level or range of sounds' loudness

- **Style**—the distinguishing characteristics and performance practices of a piece of music (classical, hip-hop, country, folk, blues, rock, jazz, reggae, and so on)

As you plan activities involving music and movement during STEM experiences, consider this guidance from the National Core Arts Standards for prekindergarten students. These standards for music and dance performance are presented as learning goals that can be directly and informally observed during the course of young children's experiences with music and movement in the classroom. You can use these performance standards as a helpful guide for integrated STEM and music or movement experiences as you work to help build children's foundational knowledge and creative-thinking skills.

National Coalition for Core Arts Standards. 2014. *National Core Arts Standards*. Dover, DE: State Education Agency Directors of Arts Education. http://www.nationalartsstandards.org/

Music and Movement Standards in the Classroom

General Music/Connecting

With guidance, young children will learn to do the following:

* Demonstrate how interests, knowledge, and skills relate to personal choices and intent when creating, performing, and responding to music

* Demonstrate understanding of relationships among music and other arts, other disciplines, varied contexts, and daily life

General Music/Creating

With substantial guidance, young children should have the opportunity to do the following:

* Explore and experience a variety of music

* Explore favorite musical ideas (such as movements, vocalizations, or instrumental accompaniments)

* Select and keep track of the order for performing original musical ideas, using iconic notation (such as drawing one image high on a page and another low on the page to show the change from a high pitch to a low one) and/or recording technology

* Consider personal, peer, and teacher feedback when demonstrating and refining personal musical ideas

* Share revised personal musical ideas with peers

General Music/Performing

With substantial guidance, young children should have the opportunity to do the following:

- Demonstrate and state preference for varied musical selections

- Explore and demonstrate awareness of musical contrasts

- Explore music's expressive qualities (such as voice quality, dynamics, and tempo)

- Practice and demonstrate what they like about their own performances

- Apply personal, peer, and teacher feedback to refine performances

- Perform music with expression

General Music/Responding

With substantial guidance, young children should have the opportunity to do the following:

- State personal interests and demonstrate why they prefer some music selections over others

- Explore musical contrasts

- Explore music's expressive qualities (such as voice quality, dynamics, and tempo)

- Talk about personal and expressive preferences in music

Dance/Connecting

Young children should have the opportunity to do the following:

- Recognize an emotion expressed in dance movement that is watched or performed

- Observe a dance work, identify and imitate the dance, and ask questions about the dance Show a dance movement experienced at home or elsewhere

Dance/Creating

Young children should be able to do the following:

- Respond in movement to a variety of sensory stimuli

- Find a different way to do several basic locomotor and nonlocomotor movements

- Improvise dance that starts and stops on cue

- Engage in dance experiences, moving alone or with a partner

- Respond to suggestions for changing movement through guided improvisational experiences

- Identify parts of the body and document a body shape or position by drawing a picture

Dance/Performing

Young children in the early childhood classroom should have the ability to do the following:

- Identify and demonstrate directions for moving the body in general space

- Identify speed of dance as fast or slow

- Move with opposing characteristics (such as loose/tight, light/heavy, jerky/smooth)

- Demonstrate basic full body locomotor and nonlocomotor movement and body patterning with spatial relationships

- Move in a general space and start and stop on cue while maintaining personal space

- Identify and move body parts and repeat movement upon request

- Dance for others in a designated area or space

- Use a simple prop as part of a dance

Dance/Responding

Young children should have the ability to do the following:

- Identify a movement in a dance by repeating it

- Demonstrate an observed or performed dance movement

- Observe a movement and share impressions

- Find a movement in a dance that is fun to watch, repeat it, and explain why it is fun to watch and do

Vignette for Understanding: Making Music

Mrs. Johnston's class had been working all week on creating their own sistrums—a percussion instrument first used by ancient Egyptians. Egyptian sistrums were typically shaped as an oval hoop made from clay, wood, or metal, with two horizontal rods holding movable disks. When a

sistrum was shaken like a rattle, the disks created sound as they struck the sides of the sistrum. Mrs. Johnston's class began by collecting forked tree branches on a nature walk. Once the branches were collected, Mrs. Johnston helped the students clean the branches and remove smaller stems so that the branches would be smooth enough to paint. To begin creating the sistrums, the children worked in pairs to paint their branches using bright acrylic paints. Taking turns in which one child held the branch and the other painted, Collette and Felix collaborated on one long branch. The children chose to paint their branch violet, blue, and gray. Laughing, Collette watched as Felix overlapped colors to create what he had labeled a "speckly" color.

On the final day of the project, each pair of children worked alongside Mrs. Johnston to wrap the ends of the branches with brightly colored string to create a colorful handle. Once the handles were wrapped, each pair of children chose colorful buttons and beads to string along a thread. Felix and Collette chose several large plastic buttons and a few smaller beads to

string. They spent a little time trying to decide the order of their buttons and beads because Felix was hoping to make a "loud" sistrum. When they finished stringing the buttons

and beads, Mrs. Johnston carefully tied the ends of the string to each side of the forked branch and secured it with hot glue as the children held the branch. Once it dried, the children added their new instrument to the class collection for use during whole-group times. The sistrums added new, unique sounds to the children's musical explorations.

Reflection

Felix and Collette's collaborative experience creating a sistrum reminds us of the important role that playfulness has in creative music and movement experiences. The creation of the sistrum affords many opportunities to speak informally with students about their senses, the science of sounds, and opportunities to make music. The experience was open ended, with no one right way to paint or choose the beads for sounds, which allowed the children to think creatively with the art materials.

Music and Movement across the Curriculum: Planning Tips

In early childhood classrooms, it is important to consider both space needs as well as time of day when planning movement and music experiences. Ample space will be necessary when introducing opportunities to dance and move. Additionally, music experiences with young children are highly active and can be loud, so consider the other activities taking place in your classroom or school when planning music experiences. There are natural connections between movement and the science and engineering concepts of force and motion, so classroom engineering and design centers provide rich opportunities for encouraging children to build and explore during independent investigations.

Questions for Exploration in STEM-Focused Music and Movement Experiences

Consider asking the following questions to encourage explorations with STEM-focused music and movement experiences:

- "Can you describe the sounds you hear? Are they soft or loud? Fast or slow?"

- "Why do you think that instrument sounds different than this one?"

- "Can you describe what makes the sound different?"

Movement can be challenging for children to describe in abstract terms. Showing images of children at play can help prompt children to label and describe movement:

- "What are the children doing?"

- "How does it feel to push or run?"

- "Can you show me with your own body how they are moving?"

Lesson Ideas

Dancing Ribbons

Topics:

Force, motion, fine and gross motor movement, and design

Objective:

Children will participate in the creation of ribbon sticks and explore motion and movement with the sticks as they dance and move.

Materials:

Wooden sticks/dowels, 12–18" long
(1 per child)

Various lengths of ribbon, cordage, lace strips, and/or yarn

Hot-glue gun (adult use)

> **Creativity Skills:**
>
> Exploration
>
> Visualization

Overview:

Children will be creating their own ribbon sticks to use during music and movement activities. As the experience will involve the use of hot glue, it is best to work with small groups of children. It can be helpful to show the children an example of a ribbon stick before they begin to create their own, if this is their first time using one.

Activity Steps:

1. Introduce the children to the various "ribbons" they can use to create their sticks.

2. Ask them to consider how materials of different weights and lengths will react when moved during dancing.

3. Invite each child to choose the materials they want to use, and assist them in wrapping the "ribbons" around the sticks.

4. Hot glue the "ribbons" into place.

5. Once the glue has cooled, invite the children to try various movements (such as fast/slow or big/little), and introduce music of varying tempos.

Documentation:

Take notes on the children's abilities to match their actions to varying movements and tempos.

Extension Lesson:

This lesson can be extended by encouraging the children to create their own movements (for example, "What do happy/sad movements look like?") or match their movements to recorded songs.

Discovery Bottles

Topics:

Understanding matter, properties of solids and liquids, movement, and design

Objective:

Children will work in pairs to create discovery bottles focused on the movement of various materials.

Materials:

Plastic water bottles (empty with labels removed)

Cooking oil

Mineral oil

Clear hand soap

Water

Food coloring

Small buttons, beads, sequins, rocks, shells, and/or glitter

Plastic funnel

Super Glue (adult use)

Overview:

Clean the bottles and remove the labels prior to beginning the activity with the children. This lesson will work best if children work in pairs or small groups to create bottles that can be used by all students in the classroom.

Activity Steps:

1. Invite the children to explore the materials you've gathered for the bottles. Talk with them about movement and encourage them to think about what might happen with the different materials. Prompting questions to ask can include the following: "What will sink faster in the bottle, a rock or a seashell? Why do you think that?", "What will

happen if we add water and mineral oil to the same bottle? Will they mix together?", "Will the cooking oil react the same way the mineral oil did?", and "Will the glitter float in water? What about in the mineral oil?"

2. Assist the students in adding their chosen liquids to their bottles and then invite them to add their chosen materials (a funnel may be useful when using a bottle with a small opening). Encourage the students to pay close attention as they add materials.

3. Once everything has been added, seal the bottle tops permanently with Super Glue.

4. Shake and observe. **Teacher tip**: Adding a few drops of clear hand soap will make objects move faster in water, while a few tablespoons of clear glue will help slow down movements. If you are using objects that are metal, mineral oil will prevent rusting.

Documentation:

Take anecdotal notes on the children's observations of movement. Be sure to encourage them to describe the movements they see.

Extension Lesson:

While this lesson targets movement, discovery bottles can be created that link to other areas of science and the arts. For example, a magnet bottle can be created with magnet chips, magnet wands, and mineral oil.

STEM Chants and Fingerplays

Topics:

Integrating STEM content, fine motor movement, and music

Objective:

Children will participate in group STEM songs and fingerplays as a way to extend their hands-on learning experiences.

Materials:

None are needed, but you may wish to create flannel-board cutouts or add musical instruments.

Creativity Skills:

Exploration

Visualization

Communication/
Collaboration

Overview:

Invite the whole class to join you for group time. Ask questions such as "Can you describe different types of movement (fast/slow, straight/curved, steady/jerky)?" to prompt the children to share their understanding of movement. Choose one chant from the following and work alongside the students to create movements to match the words or intent of the song.

Flowers Tall and Small (Life Science)— original author unknown

Flowers tall, (hold up the pointer, middle, and ring fingers)
Flowers small, (hold up the little finger and thumb)
Count them one by one, (use other hand to count each finger)
Blowing with the breezes (wave fingers slowly)
In the springtime sun! (hold all fingers straight and tall)
1, 2, 3, 4, 5 (touch each finger as you count)

Blast Off! (Earth and Space Science)— original author unknown

Climb aboard the spaceship; (climb up a ladder by moving your arms and legs)

We're going to the moon. (point to the moon in the sky)

Hurry and get ready; (run in place)

We're going to blast off soon. (continue pumping arms and legs)

Put on your helmet (put on an imaginary helmet)

And buckle up real tight, (pull imaginary seatbelt across your waist and
   snap into place)

Because here comes the countdown, (place finger in front of lips and
   make shushing noise)

So count with all your might! (count down from ten, using fingers
   to count)

Blast off! (jump into the air)

Gray Elephants Balancing (Life Science)— original author unknown

One gray elephant balancing (invite one child to move to the center and
   balance himself while pretending to walk on an imaginary string with
   outstretched arms)

Step by step on a piece of string (take careful steps in a straight line)

Thought it was such a wonderful stunt (continue carefully walking
   the line)

That he called for another elephant. (point to another child to join in
   walking the line)

Two gray elephants balancing (repeat previous actions or encourage
   children to hold hands while moving)

Step by step on a piece of string

Thought it was such a wonderful stunt

That they called for another elephant. (point to a third child to join in;
   repeat until all of the children are balancing on the "string")

(Number of children) gray elephants balancing (all children balance on
   one leg with outstretched arms)

Step by step on a piece of string. (all children take slow, careful steps
   forward)

All of a sudden the piece of string broke (all children fall to the floor)

And down came all the "ele-folk."

Documentation:

Take anecdotal notes on children's movements and cooperation during the songs. You may also wish to video their movements during these whole-group times for additional documentation.

Extension Lesson:

Additional songs and fingerplays describing movement can be added regularly throughout the school year to extend the lesson. You can also encourage the children to develop new actions for familiar songs.

Moving Möbius

Topics:

Integrating geometry, visual arts, and fine motor movement

Objective:

Children will participate in the creation of a Möbius strip and explore movement through twisting the strip and observing the outcome.

Creativity Skills:
Exploration
Visualization

Materials:

1 strip of construction paper (12" x 2")

Tape

Scissors (adult use)

Overview:

The Möbius strip is a one-sided surface with no boundaries and looks like an infinite loop. A Möbius strip has only one side, so an ant crawling along it would wind along both the bottom and the top in a single stretch. When the surface of the loop is cut in half, the loop doubles in size rather than breaking into two separate loops. For this lesson, the children will use fine motor movements to twist the strip, but they will also be challenged to think about the movement inherent to the strip itself by imagining an ant walking along the strip or by tracing the center of the strip with their own fingers. This lesson can be done with a whole group, and then the strips can be placed in the math or STEM center for children to investigate independently.

Activity Steps:

1. Ask the children to describe the shape of a circle and imagine what would happen if they twisted that circle. What would it look like?

2. To create a Möbius strip, draw a line lengthwise down the center of one 12" x 2" strip of paper.

3. Have a child hold the strip and bring the two ends together to make a loop. Invite the child to add a single half twist to  one side of the strip, and then tape the ends together. You will have an infinite loop with only one side. Run your finger along the line that you drew to show the children the surface space.

4. Carefully begin cutting on the line (begin by poking the scissors through the paper to only cut the line). When cut, the loop will grow in size.

5. Invite the children to think about how that happened from just one strip of paper. You can introduce the term *surface* to the children and ask them to think about an ant traveling along the loop—the ant will need to continually walk, as there is no end.

Documentation:

Your informal conversations with the children while making the Möbius strip and while they explore the strip can serve as a means to support their questioning.

This lesson can be extended by showing children Möbius-strip artworks made by artists. Visit the Google Arts and Culture website and search for *mobius*. https://www.google.com/culturalinstitute/beta/

Some child-friendly artworks to view on the site include the following:

Mobius by Masami Kodama. This artwork is housed at the James A. Michener Art Museum and is a large bronze outdoor sculpture.

Möbius Strip by Hiroshi Seto. This artwork is housed at the Tottori Prefectural Museum and is a ceramic sculpture.

Painted Sistrum

Topics:

Integrating sound, visual arts, and design

Objective:

Children will participate in the creation of painted sistrums and explore the sounds that can be made by playing the instruments.

Materials:

Short forked sticks (cleaned, with offshoots removed)

Variety of tempera paint colors and paintbrushes

Variety of colored cordage or yarn (each instrument will require an 18" piece)

Thin wire or strong string (such as fishing line)

Small beads and buttons (each instrument will require 5 to 8 beads or buttons)

Creativity Skills:

Exploration

Visualization

Communication/ Collaboration

Originality

Flexibility

Strategic planning

Hot-glue gun (adult use)

Scissors (adult use for cutting cordage, string, and wire)

Video-recording device

Overview:

This project will take several days to complete and works best when children work in pairs so they can help each other hold the stick during painting, wrapping, and stringing beads. You can gather the materials ahead of time or invite the students to join you on a nature walk to locate forked sticks if your location allows.

Activity Steps:

1. It may be helpful to show the children an image of a sistrum and talk about how they are used to make music by shaking.

2. Place students in pairs and encourage them to paint their sticks to make them unique.

3. Put the sticks aside to dry completely.

4. Once the sticks dry, provide each pair of children with an eighteen-inch piece of cordage or yarn to wrap around the stick to create a colorful handle. You can glue or hot glue one end down so that the children can easily wrap the handle.

5. Once each pair has the handle wrapped, glue down the other end of the cordage to keep it in place.

6. To string the beads and buttons, tie a large knot at one end of each piece of wire or fishing line and invite each pair of children to string five to eight beads or buttons.

7. Tie each beaded line across the fork of appropriate stick and secure with hot glue.

8. Invite the children to shake and rattle their new instruments to explore the sounds they can create.

Documentation:

As this is a multiday project, you will have many opportunities to observe and document children's experiences. You can take anecdotal notes on children's fine-motor, communication, and collaboration skills during the creation phase of the project and video the children as they play their sistrums.

Extension Lesson:

This lesson can be extended by inviting the children to create other instruments using familiar materials, including flutes made from plastic straws, timpani drums made from metal cans, and kazoos made from cardboard tubes.

Children's Books

Carle, Eric. 1996. *I See a Song*. New York, NY: Scholastic.

Eric Carle's engaging images in *I See a Song* feature a collection of colorful shapes and a musician and his violin.

Empson, Jo. 2012. *Rabbityness*. Auburn, ME: Child's Play.

Rabbityness is a beautifully illustrated book that moves from black-and-white minimalism to bright abstract artwork to tell of Rabbit's interesting activities and of their emotional impact for the reader.

Martin, Bill, Jr., and John Archambault. 1988. *Listen to the Rain*. New York, NY: Henry Holt and Co.

Listen to the Rain features paintings with an abstract quality and lyrical, rhyming text to encourage your students to focus their imaginations on the sounds that a single raindrop can make.

2

Connecting the Dramatic Arts to STEM

The inclusion of drama as a medium for learning and expression is a natural addition to every early childhood classroom. As children engage in dramatic-arts experiences, they have opportunities to build their skills in communication, collaboration, and creative thinking by engaging their imaginations with teacher support and guidance.

Creative drama experiences are actions, improvisations, and animated explorations developed and enacted by the children themselves. Drama experiences allow children the freedom to try out new ideas and identities, which can also build their social and emotional skills. The integration of the dramatic-arts and STEM content allows children to explore problems and ideas in novel ways that can extend their thoughts and understanding. Key terms in the dramatic arts include the following:

- **Dialogue**—the conversation of characters in a play or story

- **Plot**—the sequence of events that make up a story from beginning to end

- **Props**—objects that are used during a play or storytelling experience. Props can be abstract or concrete representations of objects.

- **Scene**—used to show the audience a change in time or a change in location or to introduce new characters.

- **Improv**—a genre of the theater arts that refers to a piece of music or story that is created on the fly, without preparation. The use of improv during group storytelling or music experiences helps to promote children's communication, critical-thinking, collaboration, and creativity skills.

As you plan activities involving the dramatic arts during STEM experiences, consider this guidance from the National Core Arts Standards for prekindergarten students. These theater performance standards are presented as learning goals that can be directly and informally observed during the course of young children's experiences with the dramatic arts in the classroom. You can use these performance standards as a helpful guide for integrated STEM and dramatic-arts experiences as you work to help build children's foundational knowledge and creative-thinking skills.

National Coalition for Core Arts Standards. 2014. *National Core Arts Standards*. Dover, DE: State Education Agency Directors of Arts Education. http://www.nationalartsstandards.org/

Theater/Connecting

With prompting and support, young children should be able to do the following:

- Identify similarities between a story and personal experience in dramatic play or a guided drama experience

- Use skills and knowledge from other areas in dramatic play or a guided drama experience

- Identify stories that are similar in dramatic play or a guided drama experience

- Tell a short story in dramatic play or a guided drama experience

Theater/Creating

With prompting and support, young children should be able to do the following:

- Transition between imagination and reality in dramatic play or a guided drama experience

- Use nonrepresentational materials to create props, puppets, and costume pieces for dramatic play or a guided drama experience

- Contribute, through gestures and words, to dramatic play or a guided drama experience

- Express original ideas in dramatic play or a guided drama experience

- Answer questions in dramatic play or a guided drama experience

Theater/Performing

With prompting and support, young children should be able to do the following:

- Identify characters in dramatic play or a guided drama experience

- Understand that imagination is fundamental to dramatic play or a guided drama experience

- Explore and experiment with various technical elements in dramatic play or a guided drama experience

- Engage in dramatic play or a guided drama experience

Theater/Responding

With prompting and support, young children should be able to do the following:

- Recall an emotional response in dramatic play or a guided drama experience

- Explore preferences in dramatic play or a guided drama experience

- Name and describe characters in dramatic play or a guided drama experience

- Actively engage in dramatic play or a guided drama experience.

Vignette for Understanding: Incorporating Drama

Mr. Davis is working closely with his class of five-year-olds to prepare for their fall field trip to the apple orchard. The class has been learning about apples all week—making applesauce, printing with apples, exploring the insides of apples to learn about seeds—and Mr. Davis has a whole-group activity planned for the children to incorporate drama and movement into their studies of the apple. During whole-group time, Mr. Davis announces, "We will be acting out a short story about the changes an apple tree goes through as it grows from a seed to a tree. We are going to work together to create the actions that go along with the story." First, Mr. Davis reads the short story "The Apple Tree" to the children. Then he explains that he is going to read the story again and invites the class to create movements for each part of the story. As he reads each line, he invites the children to present ideas for movement. When the class comes to an agreement on which suggested movement captures the intent of the story, he moves on to the next line.

After all lines have associated movements, Mr. Davis slowly reads "The Apple Tree" a third time and encourages the children to perform the movements.

The Apple Tree

- It is a warm day in autumn, and you are a ripe, red apple that has fallen to the ground. (Possible action: Curl your body up into a tight ball.)

- The warm days are gone, and now you are covered with cold snow. The snow pushes your seeds into the soil below you. (Possible action: As you lie in a ball, cover your head with your hands.)

- The days begin to warm again, and snow is replaced by spring rain. You begin to grow a root that pushes into the warm soil below you. (Possible action: As you lie in a ball, push one leg out behind you.)

- The sun is warm, and you begin to spout a tender, green seedling that pushes through the soil above you. (Possible action: Slowly stand up and push your arms above your head with your feet firmly planted.)

- Many years have passed, and now you are a tall apple tree with strong roots and long branches. Your branches have small pink flowers that are just beginning to grow. (Possible action: Stand tall and stretch out your arms.)

- In the warm spring sun, your pink flower petals fall to the ground, and small fruits just beginning to grow are left in their place. (Possible action: Move arms and float to the ground, come back to a standing place to stand tall as a tree again.)

- All summer the fruits on your branches grow heavy as they change from green to bright red. (Possible action: Lower outstretched arms.)

- In the fall, friends come every day to pick your delicious fruits. Possible action: Encourage children to take turns pretending to pick apples from classmates as they stand like trees.)

Reflection

By creating a space for his students to connect their science understanding with movement and drama, Mr. Davis is providing meaningful ways to encourage his students to extend and deepen their understanding. Inviting children to engage in movement and drama experiences will also serve to create a classroom environment where multiple ways of learning are accepted and encouraged. Young children need educators who support the many ways that young children create meaning through kinesthetic explorations, play, and dramatics. Encouraging meaningful dramatic and movement opportunities in your classroom will support children as they engage in multimodal ways of knowing, exploring, creating, and re-creating.

The Dramatic Arts across the Curriculum: Planning Tips

Drama experiences can take place at all times of the day, in all areas of the classroom and outdoors, and across all of the STEM content areas. You can also intentionally plan and support the integration of drama while children are working in STEM content, as Mr. Davis did with his students while reading "The Apple Tree." The lessons that follow will provide specific examples of drama and STEM integration, but you can restructure your classroom to support the children's spontaneous work as well. By including dramatic-play materials, your science and math centers can extend children's explorations. For example, children can use animal puppets in the science center to extend what they are learning about animals and their habitats in life science. Instead of introducing a new math lesson with a picture book on counting, you can encourage the children to join you in the creation of an improvisational story about counting.

Questions for Exploration in STEM-Focused Dramatic-Arts Experiences

The following questions can be used to encourage explorations with STEM-focused dramatic-arts experiences:

- "What story could we tell about this idea?"

- "How do you think a tiger sounds when he's happy? How does a tiger sound when he's tired?"

- "What props could you use to help tell this story? Can we create what you need?"

Creative Investigations in Early Art

- "Can you imagine what the inside of a bear's cave feels like?"

- "Imagine that you could shrink down to be teeny tiny like an ant and you could crawl inside of lots of places. How do you think it sounds inside of a computer? Is it loud or quiet? What noises would you hear if you were inside?"

Lesson Ideas

Altered Blocks: Prop Making

Topics:

Life science: human or animal habitats; dramatic arts: prop making

Objective:

Children will participate in the design and creation of dramatic-play props to add to the classroom's block-center/math-center materials.

Materials:

Wooden blocks of varying sizes and shapes

Acrylic paints of various colors

Thin paintbrushes

Permanent markers

Tape

Paper tablecloth

Painting smocks

Pictures of various habitats for people (city, countryside, neighborhood, and so on) or animals (woodlands, deserts, and so on)

Creativity Skills:

Exploration

Visualization

Communication/
Collaboration

Solution finding

Flexibility

Elaboration

Originality

Strategic planning

Overview:

This lesson will permanently alter the blocks used, so be sure to only provide blocks or building materials that can be altered. This type of experience provides children with an introduction to prop making that can easily extend their play experiences in the classroom. It will work best if children work together in small groups to create block props around a singular theme.

Activity Steps:

1. Invite the children to think about which habitat they are most interested in; you may want to offer suggestions based on their play experiences in your classroom.

2. As a class, select one habitat. Encourage the children to think about how they could paint/color their plain wooden blocks to help create props to represent buildings or trees in the chosen habitat. Encourage children to look through images of their chosen habitat. What could they do with a block to create the image of a building? How could they add windows or bricks to a block?

3. Invite your students to explore the paints and markers you have available for them. As acrylic paints and permanent markers are not washable, be sure to cover the table where the children are working and have the children wear smocks to cover their clothes. Be sure to emphasize that the children need to take care of these materials, as they are special for this project.

4. As the children work, talk with them about their choices and encourage them to refer to the habitat images for inspiration.

5. Once the blocks are completely dry, they can be added to the classroom for regular use.

Documentation:

Take anecdotal notes about the children's ability to collaborate, communicate, and create props related to the selected idea.

Extension Lesson:

This lesson can be extended by encouraging prop making in other areas of the classroom. Children can work to create images for flannel-board stories or to create puppets for storytelling.

Family Puppets

Topics:

Life science: animals and plants; dramatic arts: prop making and storytelling

Objective:

Children will create their own animal- or plant-family puppets and develop brief stories to use with their puppets.

Materials:

Felt-puppet hands (these can be made by tracing the outline of a child's hand and adding at least an inch around the hand for gluing—two 7–8" squares of felt per child)

Materials for decorating (construction paper, clay, buttons, sequins, ribbon, pipe cleaners, googly eyes, markers, tempera paints)

Scissors (adult use)

Creativity Skills:

Visualization

Communication/ Collaboration

Flexibility

Elaboration

Originality

Strategic planning

Hot-glue gun (adult use)

Sketch paper and pencils

Video-recording device

Overview:

This lesson can take place in small- or whole-group settings and can be split across several days to allow the children to plan, create, and use their puppets in storytelling. Trace, cut out, and glue the felt-puppet hands and let them dry prior to beginning the activity with the children.

Activity Steps:

1. Talk with the children about puppets. Have they used puppets in the past? Are there puppets in the classroom? What stories can they tell with puppets?

2. Introduce the idea of a family. What does *family* mean? Who is in the children's families?

3. Invite the children to think about making flower- or animal-family puppets. Encourage them to sketch out their ideas on paper. You can ask prompting questions, such as the following, to help with their plans:

   - "How many flowers will be in your family?"

   - "What will the dogs in your family look like? What color will they be?"

   - "What will you need to make the flower family?"

   - "What is a fun story about your animal or plant family that you can tell using your puppet?"

4. Once children have created their plans, invite them to begin decorating their puppets to show the families they have created. Remind them that you are available to hot glue their decorations to the felt, which will help heavier objects stay in place.

5. Once the puppets have dried, set up a location in the classroom for storytelling with puppets, or use whole-group time for children to share their stories.

Documentation:

The sketches and puppets can be used to document the children's experiences and understanding of the related science concepts. You can video or take anecdotal notes during the children's storytelling to document their related communication and expressive experiences.

Extension Lesson:

This lesson can be extended by inviting the children to create puppets of their actual families; this type of experience could be fun to complete with their families during a family-event night at your school.

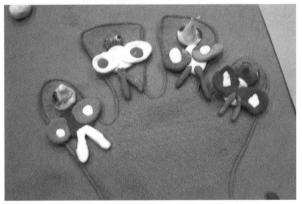

Digital Storytelling

Topics:

Technology use; dramatic arts: storytelling

Objectives:

Children will use digital media to communicate and work collaboratively.

Creativity Skills:

Exploration

Communication/ Collaboration

Documentation

Children will use digital media to communicate clearly and express themselves verbally and visually.

Materials:

iPad or tablet for children's use, with apps loaded

Creative, free apps available for iPad and Android platforms include the following:

- Lipa Theater: Story Maker, by Lipa Learning. Recommended ages: 4 and up. This app allows children to create and record stories in a digital puppet theater.

- Yumi Story Dice Kids, by AACorn. Recommended ages: 4 and up. This app is a choose-your-own adventure, in which a roll of the dice can change the direction of your story.

- StoryBots, by JibJab Media, Inc. Recommended ages: 3 and up. This app has many books and videos and even has the ability for children to star in their own stories.

Overview:

This lesson works best if children work in pairs during app play to promote collaboration and communication.

Activity Steps:

1. If this is the first time using a particular app, it is a good idea to briefly introduce the app and its various functions during whole-group time so that the children have an idea of what a particular app can do.

2. Invite a pair of children to choose an app to create with during their time in the technology center. Questions such as "What happened when you did _____?", "Do you know how to make _____ happen?", and "Why did _____ happen when you did _____?" can help to promote intentionality in their actions.

3. As documentation is an important component of any digital play, ask the children to share their experiences with storytelling with the class during whole-group time.

Documentation:

Take anecdotal notes about the children's ability to collaborate, communicate, and create stories.

Group documentation can include the story itself as a means to document the ways in which children expressed their understanding and ideas.

Extension Lesson:

Digital video can also be introduced as a form of collaborative storytelling in your classroom, and those videos can be shared with families.

Guided Imagery with Children

Topics:

Life science, earth science, and the dramatic arts

Objective:

Children will participate in guided-imagery stories to promote visualization and imaginative thinking.

Creativity Skills:

Exploration

Visualization

Originality

Materials:

None are needed.

Overview:

Guided imagery can be done with small or whole groups of children, but be sure to have room for the children to sit or lie down to relax. You will also want to find a relatively quiet space or time during the day so that your students will be able to focus on your words and the images you associate with the stories you share.

Activity Steps:

1. Ask the children to close their eyes and think about a dog. Can they tell you what their pet dogs look like? Are they big or small? Do their tails wag?

2. Ask the children to open their eyes, and talk with them about *imagination*. Have they heard that word before? Can they talk about a time when they used their imaginations?

3. Explain that you are going to read an imagery story and invite the children to close their eyes and try to imagine the pictures that go along with the story. Encourage the children to get comfortable and recommend that they be as quiet as possible.

4. After you complete an imagery story, invite the children to share their experiences. If guided imagery is new to your students, you may want to repeat this activity over several days with different stories so that the children become accustomed to the process.

Choose one of the following guided-imagery stories to experience with the class. The original authors for these stories are unknown:

Walking in the Snow

1. Find a place in the room where you can lie down and stretch out or sit very still.

2. Take two or three slow, deep breaths and see if you can be very, very still. Listen to your breathing and see if you can breathe so quietly that no one can hear you.

3. Try to relax, but be sure to keep your back straight so you can breathe better.

4. Close your eyes and let your imagination make a picture of a beautiful, snowy day.

5. Use your imagination to put on your coat and boots and walk outside

into the fluffy, white snow. Have you ever walked in the snow before? Feel the snow as it falls gently on your hands and face. Hold out your hands until they are full of snow.

6. Look at the snow you are holding in your hands and open your fingers and let the snow fall back to the ground. A gentle breeze blows the snow all around you, feeling fresh and cool and good. Imagine that you are walking in the snow. It feels crunchy and your boots make little sounds as you walk around. You find a nice place where the snow is very fluffy. Lie down and use your arms and legs to make snow angels. Look at your snow angels. You feel very happy playing in the snow and making angels.

7. You are beginning to feel a little cold, so it is time to come inside where it is nice and warm. You are thinking about something warm to drink. Imagine what you would like to have to drink when you get inside. Think about our room and see if you can make a picture of it in your mind.

8. When you are ready to stop playing in the snow, listen to the sounds you hear in our room. Wiggle your fingers and give your body a nice long stretch. Open your eyes and look around until you see me.

The Forest

1. Find a place in the room where you can lie down and stretch out or sit very still.

2. Take two or three slow, deep breaths and see if you can be very, very still. Listen to your breathing and see if you can breathe so quietly that no one can hear you. Try to relax, but be sure to keep your back straight so you can breathe better.

3. Now imagine that you are walking down a path into a green forest. As you walk along the path, you take in the sights, sounds, smells, and feel of the trees and plants. All around you are trees, grasses, ground cover, and fragrant flowers. You hear the soothing sounds of birds chirping and the wind as it gently blows through the treetops. Through gaps in the treetops, you see the sun high in a cloudless, blue sky. The

sunlight is coming through the canopy of the treetops and filters down onto the forest floor, creating beautiful patterns of light and shadow.

4. You soon come to a clearing in the forest, where there are no trees. There are several flat rocks in the clearing surrounded by soft moss. A small stream runs among the rocks. You lie back on one of the rocks or on the cushiony moss and put your feet into the cool water. You feel the warm sun and a gentle, light breeze through your hair and across your skin. The sparkling, clear water rushes around the multicolored rocks. You put your hand into the water and lift a handful to your lips. The water is cool and refreshing. You close your eyes and listen to the water trickling around the rocks.

5. When you are ready, imagine that you slowly get up and leave the clearing. As you walk back down the path through the forest, you can feel the warm sunlight on your face. When you are ready to stop walking in the forest, listen to the sounds you hear in our room. Wiggle your fingers and give your body a nice long stretch. Open your eyes and look around until you see me.

The Beach

1. Find a place in the room where you can stretch out or sit very quietly. Take two or three slow, deep breaths and see if you can be very, very still. Listen to your breathing and see if you can breathe so quietly that no one can hear you. Try to relax, but be sure to keep your back straight so you can breathe better.

2. Imagine you are walking down a long, narrow wooden stairway toward a beautiful beach with lots of sand. Your bare feet feel the rough, weathered steps, and you notice how the white sand stretches down the shoreline as far as you can see. The ocean is a bright shade of blue, with many waves sweeping toward the shore. You reach the end of the stairway and step down, sinking into the warm sand. As you rub the sand lightly between your toes, you bend down to pick up a handful of sand. What does the sand feel like between your fingers and toes?

3. You begin walking slowly toward the edge of the water and notice the warm sun on your face and shoulders. The salty sea air smells good, and you take in a deep breath . . . breathe slowly out . . . and feel more relaxed and refreshed. Finally, you reach the water's edge, and you step into the water and watch it flow over your toes and ankles. You watch the waves glide smoothly toward you, gently sweeping around your feet, and the trails of seawater flow slowly back out again. The cool water feels soft and comforting as you look out at the ocean in front of you. Overhead, you notice two seagulls gracefully soaring high above the ocean waters, and you can hear their soft cries becoming faint as they fly away.

4. After a moment, you begin walking down the beach at the water's edge. As you continue your leisurely walk down the beach, you notice a colorful beach chair resting in a nice, peaceful spot where the powdery, soft sand is very smooth. You approach this comfortable-looking beach chair, then you sit down, lie back, and settle in. You take in a long, deep breath, breathe slowly out, and feel even more relaxed and comfortable resting in your chair. When you are ready to stop resting in your chair, listen to the sounds you hear in our room. Wiggle your fingers and give your body a nice long stretch. Open your eyes and look around until you see me.

Documentation:

Anecdotal notes on children's experiences with guided imagery can be collected as they discuss their experiences.

Extension Lesson:

This lesson can be extended by creating guided-imagery stories that align with the earth- or life-science topics you cover in the classroom—a walk in space, flying in an airplane looking at the earth, or viewing animals in the wild.

Children's Books

Daywalt, Drew. 2013. *The Day the Crayons Quit.* New York, NY: Philomel Books.

The Day the Crayons Quit shares a fanciful story of the untold lives of crayons that will engage your students and invite them to think about how everyday items can be exciting when used to tell unexpected stories.

Kelsey, Elin, and Soyeon Kim. 2012. *You Are Stardust.* Toronto, ON: Owlkids Books.

You Are Stardust provides children with many opportunities to use their creativity and imaginations as they explore beautiful diorama art that is presented in the text. The book does a great job of inviting children to think about the ways we are all connected to the natural world.

Williams, Sue. 1996. *I Went Walking.* Boston, MA: HMH Books for Young Readers.

This engaging board book tells of a young boy's walk through the countryside. The book slowly introduces each animal that he encounters, which invites children to take part in the story by guessing which animal will appear next.

3
Connecting the Visual Arts to STEM

As a child uses clay to build a bridge, she is learning not only about the properties of clay and working with clay but also about the engineering concepts of balance, uprightness, and symmetry. Integrated experiences in the visual arts and STEM can provide your students with many opportunities to find meaning in the work they are doing with science, technology, engineering, and mathematics. However, experiences in the visual arts are more diverse than mere opportunities to make art. A comprehensive model of early childhood visual-arts education

includes art-making experiences, opportunities for encounters with art, and aesthetic experiences (Eglinton, 2003). Attention to all three model components will help support children's skill and knowledge development in the visual arts and in the STEM disciplines.

Eglinton, Kristen. 2003. *Art in the Early Years.* New York, NY: Routledge.

Key Terms in the Visual Arts

Media—materials that are used to create a work of art; common media that are used in early childhood classrooms are tempera paints, watercolor paints, clay, pastels, colored pencils, and markers. Digital media include cameras that are used in arts experiences or for documentation.

Expression—expressive characteristics of art

Aesthetic—considerations of beauty or the appreciation of beauty

Narrative—art that tells a story

As you plan activities involving the visual arts and STEM experiences, consider this guidance from the National Core Arts Standards for prekindergarten students. These visual-arts performance standards are presented as learning goals that can be directly and informally observed during the course of young children's experiences with visual arts in the classroom. You can use these performance standards as a helpful guide for integrated STEM and visual-arts experiences as you work to help build children's foundational knowledge and creative-thinking skills.

National Coalition for Core Arts Standards. 2014. *National Core Arts Standards.* Dover, DE: State Education Agency Directors of Arts Education. http://www.nationalartsstandards.org/

Core Ideas in Visual Arts

Visual Arts/Connecting

As children work in the visual arts, they will learn to do the following:

- Explore the world using descriptive and expressive words and art making

- Recognize that people make art

- Engage in self-directed play with materials

- Engage in self-directed, creative making

- Use a variety of art-making tools

- Share materials with others

- Create and tell about art that communicates a story about a familiar place or object

- Share and talk about personal artwork

Visual Arts/Presenting

During visual-arts experiences, children will learn to do the following:

- Identify reasons for saving and displaying objects, artifacts, and artwork

- Identify places where art may be displayed or saved

- Identify where art is displayed both inside and outside of school

- Recognize art in one's environment

- Distinguish between images and real objects

- Interpret art by identifying and describing subject matter

- Select a preferred artwork

Vignette for Understanding: Reclaimed Artworks in the Community

Asia and her class on are a special field trip to the Virginia Zoo. In addition to seeing the animals, the children are going to see a sculpture in the children's garden. Asia is very excited because the class is going to look at the sculpture that is made from reclaimed and recycled materials and then make their own sculpture for their new class garden when they get back to school. They have been exploring all about the environment and why recycling is important.

As they come to the children's garden, Mr. Eric, the class teacher, calls out, "All right, kids, this is the children's garden, and you can see all kinds of recycled materials used in here. Take a walk around, but stay right in this area with your partner and tell us when you find a recycled material." Asia and her partner are standing right beside a tire painted bright yellow with flowers planted inside it. Asia calls out, "Mr. Eric, look at the tire!" Several of her classmates and Mr. Eric walk in for a closer look, while other children note that they see other tires with flowers nearby. "Well, look at that," says Mr. Eric. "Did you ever think about planting flowers in a tire?"

As the class explores, they make their way to a large sculpture in the middle of the garden that is shaped like a tree and is made with recycled bottles. As the children look, Mr. Eric talks about how the artist designed the sculpture and asks, "What do you think it looks like?" Asia immediately calls out, "A tree," and Mr. Eric asks her why she thinks that. Asia points to the long pieces of metal that have bottles on the ends and says that they are the tree limbs and that the bigger piece of metal in the center is the trunk. Mr. Eric acknowledges Asia's ideas and goes on to encourage the children to think about why the artist made a sculpture of a tree to go in a garden. The children begin to call out their ideas, and Mr. Eric encourages each child to explain his or her thoughts and observations.

Reflection

On-site or museum visits are not the only means for exposing children to the visual-art world. Many communities have installed public artworks in parks, zoos, and nature centers and on the grounds of community and municipal buildings. Often these are works that we pass by every day but fail to visually and aesthetically explore. Drawing young children's attention to the public visual art found within their own communities can be a positive way to build their understanding of their communities and the role of the arts within those communities. Knowing about the locations of community artworks can encourage teachers to introduce more art-viewing experiences.

Integrating the Visual Arts across the Curriculum: Planning Tips

Interactions with the visual arts can involve many different types of materials and media. Creating a classroom arts center, or specifically a visual-arts center, is a good pedagogical strategy for encouraging children to create and explore during independent investigations. Ample space will be a necessary consideration when planning your arts center because children will need space to plan out and create with various media and because there will need to be designated drying and storage areas. Such a center can house paper of various sizes and weights, easels, various types of paint, brushes, clay, clay tools, craft sticks, tape, rubber bands, art books and posters, sketch paper, visual-arts journals, pencils, and pens. Electronic media such as digital cameras, iPads, or tablets can also be included in the visual-arts center for children to use to create or research their ideas or questions.

Questions for Arts Explorations

The following questions can be used to encourage guided explorations with the visual arts and STEM disciplines:

- "What is the first thing you notice about this artwork?"

- "Have you ever seen an artwork like this before?"

- "Why do you think the artist made this artwork?"

- "What kinds of materials were used to make this?"

- "How did you decide what to draw/paint/create?"

- "Can you tell me about what you've drawn/painted/created?"

Lesson Ideas

Plan and Plant a Color Garden

Topics:

Life science: plant growth and change; visual arts: color and expression

Objective:

Children will participate in the planning, planting, and caretaking of a classroom color garden.

Materials for Planning Phase:

Sketch paper

Pencils

Flower images to cut

Child-safe scissors

Tape or glue

A large piece of construction paper or presentation board to create the final garden layout

iPad or tablet for research

Creativity Skills:

Exploration

Visualization

Strategic planning

Documentation

Communication/
Collaboration

Materials for Planting Phase:

Seeds or seedlings for the chosen flowers

Containers (if container gardening)

Soil (if container gardening)

Materials for making signs (tempera paints, paintbrushes, wooden stakes, weather-resistant boards)

Hammer and nails (adult use)

Trowels or small shovels

Watering cans or containers

Materials for Caretaking (Growth) Phase:

Watering cans or containers

Science or art journals

Pencils

Rulers (to measure growth)

Overview:

This experience will take place over the course of several months, so it is important to understand that children's individual interests will wax and wane over the course of the project. Provide each child the space to engage during the times she is interested, and during the times she is less interested in taking an active role, encourage her to observe and listen to her peers describing the observed changes.

Activity Steps:

Planning Phase:

1. Encourage the children to describe all the colors of flowers they've seen growing in gardens or in stores. Invite the class to recall the

primary colors (red, yellow, and blue) and secondary colors (green, orange, and violet).

2. Talk with the children about planting a color garden—a garden that has primary or secondary or both colors of flowers.

3. Invite the children to spend time in the arts center or other location in which you've placed the images of flowers to create their own color-garden plans.

4. Help the children use the iPad or tablet to research the names or varieties of the flowers they've chosen. Invite the class to look over the flowers and choose the favorite (or most-available) flowers to grow in your class garden. You will need to do some additional research on whether the selected varieties require full sun, partial sun, or shade and then help the children to create the final design of your garden as a class.

5. Once research has been completed, invite the children to create sketches of possible garden layouts using pencils and paper. You can also encourage them to cut out and glue or tape images of flowers from advertisements, magazines, or other sources onto their designs. If desired, the class can create a final garden layout on a larger piece of construction paper or presentation board to display.

Planting Phase:

1. Before beginning this part of the activity, nail the weather-resistant boards to the stakes to create signs.

2. Work alongside the children to paint labels on the signs for each type of flower. If individual children already know how to make some of the necessary letters, invite those children to do so. Alternatively, encourage the class to dictate the labels to you. Let the labels dry.

3. Invite the children to paint the labeled signs, reminding them to avoid painting over the words. Let the signs dry.

4. Invite the children to join you in planting the seeds or seedlings according to the design plan.

5. Once planting is complete, encourage the children to post the signs by the applicable plants.

Caretaking (Growth) Phase:

1. Invite the children to join you in watering the flowers at appropriate times.

2. Demonstrate how to measure the growth patterns of the flowers using a ruler. Encourage the children to keep track of the growth patterns in their science or art journals.

Documentation:

As a longer-term project, you will have many opportunities to observe children's thinking during your conversations and their observation sessions. In addition, their garden plans and science/art journals will provide ample evidence of their experiences and thinking during the project.

Extension Lesson:

This lesson can be extended by creating other varieties of gardens, including butterfly gardens, fruit gardens, and vegetable gardens; these are all examples of easy-to-grow gardens that can be done in large containers or small spaces around your school.

Loose-Parts Group Build

Topics:

Earth science: conservation and recycling; visual arts: sculpture and working in 3-D

Objectives:

Children will work alongside others to create an ever-changing collaborative sculpture with loose parts and found objects.

Children will explore the properties of traditional and nontraditional classroom building materials.

Materials:

Loose-parts materials (wood planks; cork; plywood; wicker; balsa-wood strips; wooden craft sticks; glass or plastic cabochons of various sizes, colors, and shapes [note: cabochons are beads with one flat side and one rounded side; they are often known as vase fillers]; stones; tiles of various sizes and shapes)

Found objects, such as parts of broken or discarded toys, materials for recycling (boxes, plastic containers), and earth materials (rocks, leaves, seashells)

Camera

Overview:

This lesson can remain in your classroom for several days or weeks, depending on student interest, so it is a good idea to locate a space in your classroom where materials can be left out and children can revisit them. The idea is to teach that the creation process is ever changing and cumulative, so children need opportunities to revisit previous work.

Activity Steps:

1. Invite the children to explore the loose parts and found objects you've gathered and to think about the ways the objects and materials can be used.

2. Ask questions such as the following to help prompt the children to start exploring the ways in which objects can be combined and recombined: "What could you create with those shiny stones?" or "Do you think you could put those objects together to create something?" Help the children understand that the intent is to work together and that their groups' work will evolve and change over time.

Creativity Skills:

Exploration

Visualization

Communication/ Collaboration

Solution finding

Flexibility

Elaboration

Originality

Problem solving

Strategic planning

Creative Investigations in Early Art

3. Be sure to remind the students that they will have many opportunities to work with the materials over the coming days and weeks.

Documentation:

As this is a longer-term experience, you have many opportunities to observe and extend children's thinking and experiences if you spend time working alongside them. You can also use the camera to photograph their work. The children may wish to have a picture of a favorite creation before it is disassembled and its pieces are used in new ways.

Extension Lesson:

This lesson can be extended by adding new materials, which will help keep students interested over time and encourage them to think and create in novel ways.

Color Suncatchers

Topics:

Earth science: sun and shadow; visual arts: color

Objective:

Children will create suncatchers to explore color and the concepts of opacity and translucency.

Creativity Skills:

Exploration

Visualization

Originality

Strategic planning

Materials:

Liquid white glue (you will need about 2 ounces of glue per child)

Liquid watercolors or liquid food coloring

Toothpicks

A variety of disposable lids (plastic lids from containers of yogurt, butter, sour cream, and so on are easier to remove the dried suncatchers from) (1 lid per child)

String or ribbon for hanging suncatchers, cut into 4" pieces (1 per child)

Hole punch

Overview:

Objects that block all light are *opaque*—no one can see through these objects. Objects that let some light through are *translucent*, and these objects act as filters and only allow certain colors of light through. This lesson can be done with children working in small groups. As there are multiple steps, it will work best if you work alongside the children and help support them through each step.

Activity Steps:

1. Ask the children if they've ever seen stained glass. Can they describe what they've seen? You can also show some images of stained glass and  invite the children to think about how the light would filter through the colors on the window. Remind them of the terms *opaque* and *translucent* and invite them to create their own suncatchers that will hang in a window to block light or let light through.

2. Invite each child to pour enough glue into one of the disposable lids to cover the entire inner surface.

3. Encourage the children to choose which colors they would like to use on their suncatchers. Have the children squeeze one or two drops of each color onto the glue. The children can then use toothpicks to swirl colors together. Remind the children that, as in painting with

watercolors, the colors will turn dark if the children mix too much, so they will want to stop swirling before that happens.

4. Let the suncatchers dry. They will take about two to three days to dry completely. Invite the children to observe the suncatchers during the drying phase as the colors settle and expand into the glue. When the edges of the suncatchers are easy to peel, remove them carefully from the lids and punch a small hole through the top of each suncatcher for the children to add their string or ribbon.

5. Hang the suncatchers in an area with lots of natural light.

Documentation:

As you work alongside the children and as they observe while drying and hanging the suncatchers, you will have many opportunities to casually observe their thinking about light and color. You can make anecdotal notes from these observations.

Extension Lesson:

This lesson can be extended by repeating the activity with clear glue and encouraging the children to make transparent suncatchers to note the differences among opaque, translucent, and now transparent objects.

Melting and Mixing Colors

Topics:

Physical science: solids and liquids; earth science: reuse and conservation; visual arts: exploring primary and secondary colors

Objectives:

Children will explore their understanding of primary and secondary colors.

Children will explore the properties of solids and liquids as they work with solid and melted crayons.

Creativity Skills:

Exploration

Visualization

Strategic planning

Materials:

Small broken crayons of all colors

Silicone mini-muffin or ice-cube trays

Wooden skewers

Oven

Overview:

This lesson works best if children work in pairs or small groups. Talk with the children about the need to find ways to reuse and recycle materials. This activity is a great way for the children to reuse their broken crayons by melting and re-forming them into new, larger crayons—perhaps in colors that the children create themselves.

Activity Steps:

1. Invite children to share what they recall or know about a solid and a liquid—a *solid* has its own shape, and a *liquid* takes the shape of the container that it is in. Heating certain solids (such as crayons) will change them into liquids. The melted crayons will then take the shape of the silicone molds before hardening into new shapes.

2. Show the children the silicone trays they will be using to re-form their broken crayons into new shapes and, if they desire, new colors.

3. Invite the children to remove all wrappers on the crayon pieces before deciding which crayon pieces to put together in the individual molds to create their new crayons. **Teacher tip:** Crayon pieces of similar size will melt more evenly than if you have both large and small pieces. The melted crayons will take up less space than the solid pieces, so it is all right if pieces stick out of the tops of the molds.

4. As the children are deciding which colors to melt together, take the time to ask prompting questions about the colors they are hoping to create. For example, you might ask, "What color will you make if you add the red and blue pieces together?", "If you want to make orange,

which colors could you add to your mold?", or "How can we make that color darker or lighter?"

5. Once the molds are filled, place them into a preheated 275-degree oven.

6. Monitor crayons over a ten- to thirteen-minute period.

7. Remove the crayons from the oven and place them on a heat-resistant surface. **Safety note:** Melted crayons can be stirred with a wooden skewer to better  incorporate the colors—children should do this only under direct supervision.

8. Let crayons rest and harden over the next thirty minutes. Once they are completely cooled, invert the tray to pop the crayons out.

9. Be sure to talk to the children about the results.

Documentation:

You can take anecdotal notes on the children's understanding of recycling/reusing, solids/liquids, and primary/secondary colors.

Extension Lesson:

This lesson can be extended by challenging the children to create certain colors or shades of colors. Remember that adding black to any color will darken it and adding white will lighten it.

Shape-Walk Altered Photos

Topics:

Geometry: 2-D and 3-D shapes; visual arts: color and expression

Objectives:

Children will photograph 2-D and 3-D shapes as they walk around the school or neighborhood.

Children will recognize and name 2-D shapes (circles, triangles, rectangles, ovals, hexagons, and squares).

Children will recognize and name 3-D shapes (cube, prism, cylinder, pyramid, sphere, and cone).

Creativity Skills:

Exploration

Communication/ Collaboration

Visualization

Elaboration

Originality

Children will explore the properties of color to alter photographs of shapes.

Materials:

Camera(s)

Printed photographs (at least 4 photographs per child)

Watercolor paints

Washable markers

Glue

Scissors (adult use)

Child-safe scissors

Large sheets of paper, 1 per child (18" x 24" paper works well for this lesson)

Overview:

This experience has two main components—a shape walk, in which children will photograph the shapes they see in their environment; and an opportunity to choose photographs and alter them with markers or paints. Altering photographs in this manner allows children to experience the visual-art concept of *layering*. Layers are simultaneous, overlapping components of an image that come together to create a singular, unique image. Children will work in pairs or small groups (depending on the number of cameras available) to seek out shapes.

Activity Steps (Shape Walk):

1. Invite the children to think about the types of shapes they've seen around the classroom, school, and playground. Where have they seen a circle? A rectangle? Let them know that they will be going on a shape walk to photograph shapes, and they will use those photographs to create an artwork.

2. Invite the children to work in pairs or small groups to photograph shapes.

3. Guide the children on a walk around the school and playground. Remind them to take photographs of the shapes they see.

Activity Steps (Altering Photographs):

1. Once back in the classroom, you will need to select images to print. Involving the children at this stage can help them recall the images they've seen and take ownership of every phase of the project.

2. Set up a large table with space for a few children to work at a time. Encourage the children to look through the selections of photographs and name the shapes that they see.

3. Talk with the children about how artists can use paint or computer programs/apps to alter or change images—color can be added, and the size or shape of the image can change. Talk to the children about making a collage of photographs that they can alter using child-safe scissors, glue, markers, or paints.

4. Encourage the children to think through which images they would like to include, and allow them plenty of time to experiment with the altering process.

5. Provide the children with the arts media needed to alter their photos, and encourage them to think about why they are making the alterations by asking questions such as "Why did you decide to add yellow to that picture?", "What shape are you cutting the photo into?", "What shapes can you see in your artwork?", and "Why did you choose to include this shape?"

6. Remind the children to attach their photos to the large pieces of paper to complete their altered collages.

Documentation:

As this is a longer-term experience, you have many opportunities to observe and extend children's thinking and experiences if you spend time working alongside them. You can also use the camera to photograph their work as it evolves while they alter their photos.

Extension Lesson:

This lesson can be extended by creating altered collages of life- or earth-science concepts using photographs of a class garden or a field trip to the zoo, which will provide interesting images for children to alter and manipulate.

Children's Books

Harris, Marie. 2013. *The Girl Who Heard Colors.* New York, NY: Nancy Paulsen Books.

This engaging picture book introduces children to the idea of experiencing the world with all five senses and to individuals that can perceive the world a little differently—hearing colors or smelling words is called *synesthesia*.

Ljungkvist, Laura. 2015. *A Line Can Be* . . . New York, NY: POW! Kids Books.

This fun board book will encourage children to follow a single line from cover to cover as it forms various shapes and takes on different characteristics. The modern style of the book and the bright, patterned pages will encourage children to explore independently or with others.

Reynolds, Peter H. 2012. *Sky Color.* Somerville, MA: Candlewick.

Reynolds is the author/illustrator for two other well-loved books, *The Dot* and *Ish*. *Sky Color* carries on in this tradition by encouraging children to consider that all people can create and express themselves through art. This book will encourage children to paint what they see and observe in the world rather than someone else's ideas of what the world should look like.

4

Connecting Artists and Artworks to Investigations in STEM

The regular integration of information about artists and artworks from various genres and time periods can be used to develop a comprehensive early-childhood arts curriculum. For example, in many early childhood classrooms, children are invited to engage in marble painting or splatter painting, which are often introduced as stand-alone art-making experiences. However, by introducing the children to an artwork made with these techniques—such as *Number 1, 1949* by Jackson Pollock, influential American painter and major figure in the abstract expressionist movement—children can connect their painting techniques to those of other artists and to the ideas of color and shape that can be seen in Pollock's work. Introducing the children to an image of an artist's work and asking exploratory or focused questions can help bring meaning to the children's own art-making experiences and help connect them to the larger world of art. Art-viewing experiences connecting children to on-site or virtual museum visits can also be used create cross-curricular learning opportunities. The performing arts and artists can also be introduced, seen, and heard in early childhood classrooms through a wide variety of music- and art-sharing websites and apps.

Through the inclusion of artist studies, artworks, songs, and plays, teachers can integrate children's opportunities to create and view artworks. When children listen to a new song or view a new painting and then engage in a related art-making activity, they can connect their observations about both experiences. Learning to observe is an important skill that can be fostered through carefully designed art-viewing and art-making experiences. Teachers can help students develop observation skills by talking about the color, line, texture, and form of a piece of artwork; the sounds and tones of a piece of music; or the characters and story line of a new story or play. Gaining experience with careful observation promotes children's use of thinking and reflection skills, which will allow them to see beyond their initial impressions and explore new ideas and ways of understanding.

As your plan integrates arts and STEM experiences featuring artwork or artists, consider this guidance from the ECAE. You can use these core beliefs and values related to art education for prekindergarten students as a helpful guide to create meaningful early arts experiences with your students.

- Every child is innately curious and seeks to construct personal knowledge and understanding of the world in all of its complexity.

- Children construct knowledge in meaningful social contexts with peers and adults.

- Children experience the world in a holistic way that is best served by an interdisciplinary approach.

- Children construct insight and knowledge through guided and spontaneous learning experiences.

- The arts support multiple ways of knowing and learning that are inherent in the unique nature of each child.

- The arts empower children to communicate, represent, and express their thoughts, feelings, and perceptions.

- The arts offer opportunities to develop creativity, imagination, and flexible thinking.

- Children have a right to their cultural heritage. The arts can enrich a young child's understanding of diverse cultures.

- Early childhood art programs should be comprehensive in scope, including studio experiences, interactions with artists, visits to museums and art galleries, and opportunities to respond to art through conversation, storytelling, play, dramatics, movement, music, and art making.

National Art Education Association. n.d. *Art: Essential for Early Learning.* Position paper. Alexandria, VA: National Art Education Association. https://www.arteducators.org/community/articles/67-early-childhood-art-educators-ecae

Vignette for Understanding: The Art of Dr. Seuss and The Lorax

Mrs. White's preschool class has spent the past week reading and learning from Dr. Seuss's *The Lorax*, a classic children's book. The children have been working on a long-term project focused on caring for the environment, and the book chronicles the environmental plight of a mythical land whose Truffula trees are cut down to create special clothing. Mrs. White and her students read the book together at whole-group time, and Mrs. White invited the

children to make their own Truffula trees using clay for the bases, colorful straws as tree trunks, and brightly colored pompoms as the treetops. The children spent several afternoons making Truffula-tree forests on a long table in their classroom.

Noting the children's interest in the Truffula-tree forests, Mrs. White has decided to introduce a new version of the activity, which will encourage the children to use different media to create Truffula trees. To create the new trees, Mrs. White has included paper cones for bases and brightly colored pipe cleaners, tissue paper, ribbons, and markers to make the other parts of the trees. In the center of the arts table, she has included a few images of Truffula trees from the book so that the children can refer to them for inspiration. The children spend time glancing among the images, their own artwork, and the work of their classmates. Mrs. White reminds the students that there is no one correct way to make a Truffula tree and that they should spend time thinking about how to make their own trees come to life.

Reflection

Encouraging children to work with a variety of open-ended materials enriches children's art-making experiences by encouraging them to explore and create in new ways. Mrs. White's careful attention to her students' interests allowed her to develop experiences that draw on their prior knowledge and push their thinking in new directions. This experience integrates literacy, science, and the visual arts, which helps to support the many ways children come to understand the world around them. Young children need open-ended, materials-rich art-learning

opportunities to support their senses of inquiry and creative thinking. Because building understanding takes time and repeated interactions with ideas, continued experiences exploring new understanding and developing existing understanding are an important element of children's learning in the STEAM disciplines.

Connecting Artists and Artworks to Investigations in STEM across the Curriculum: Planning Tips

Many classic picture books contain beautiful, engaging imagery for children to explore in depth. In addition, local community art can be a great source for children to explore because of its natural connections to the community. Teachers can begin the process of locating public artwork by contacting local city councils, public arts commissions, or community arts organizations. These organizations can provide information on artwork, artists, and community arts programs in the local area. The internet provides endless opportunities to learn about many genres of art from all over the world. Many museums, centers, and galleries have partial or entire digital collections to visit online. Finally, the world of music is available at any time with apps and websites such as Pandora, Shazam, and Spotify, where teachers can create specific stations based on interests in a particular genre or artist.

Questions for STEM-Connected Artists and Artwork Explorations

Ask the following questions to encourage guided explorations of artists and their work:

- "What do you notice about this song/artwork/story?"

- "How do you feel when you look at or hear this artwork/song/story?"

- "Why would an artist create this type of artwork or song?"

- "Artists use many different types of materials to create art. What was used to create this artwork?"

- "What instruments were used to create the sounds in this song?"

Lesson Ideas

Assemblage Art—Working with Reclaimed Materials

Topics:

Earth science: conservation and recycling; visual arts: sculpture and working from 2-D to 3-D

Objectives:

Children will work together to create an ever-changing collaborative sculpture with loose parts and found objects.

Children will explore the properties of traditional and nontraditional classroom art-media materials.

Materials:

Loose-parts materials (wood planks; cork; plywood; wicker; balsa-wood strips; wooden craft sticks; glass or plastic cabochons of various sizes, colors, and shapes; stones; tiles of various sizes and shapes)

Found objects (parts of broken or discarded toys), materials for recycling (boxes, plastic containers), and earth materials (rocks, leaves, seashells)

Creativity Skills:

Exploration

Visualization

Communication/
Collaboration

Solution finding

Flexibility

Elaboration

Originality

Problem solving

Strategic planning

Lunch sacks

Tempera paints, paintbrushes, glue, tape, and markers

Hot-glue gun (adult use)

Sketch paper and pencils

Camera

iPad or tablet

Website to Explore:

Search for *assemblage art and artists* using the Google Arts and Culture site (https://www.google.com/culturalinstitute/beta/). A few child-friendly artists include the following:

> *The Brick Wall* by Douglas Coupland. This artwork is housed at the Vancouver Art Gallery and is a large assemblage piece featuring toys and toy construction pieces.

> *Constellation* by Jerzy Brzuskiewicz. This artwork is housed at the Centre of Contemporary Art Znaki Czasu and is an assemblage piece that uses everyday objects to create a constellation against a night sky.

> *Head* by Rafael Ferrer. This artwork is housed at the Art Museum of the Americas and is an assemblage piece that uses painted scrap metal to depict a colorful 3-D head sculpture.

Overview:

This lesson will take place over several days in your classroom and connect to your students' understanding of reducing, reusing, and recycling. If you are asking the children to collect loose-parts materials or found objects from home, send children home with small paper lunch sacks and encourage family members to allow the children to place items in the sacks that they can use for their artwork. You might offer the family members suggestions for possible objects, such as small broken toys, nature objects, broken crayons, plastic lids, or containers. It's important to share with family members that these objects won't be returned, so they need to ensure that they aren't sending anything of personal value.

Activity Steps:

1. With your students, look at images of assemblage artwork. Questions to prompt the discussion include the following: "What's the first thing you notice?", "What do you think this artwork is made of?", "What objects do you notice in this artwork?", and "Why would an artist use this object to make an artwork?" Introduce the idea of *reusing* to the children and talk about how artists can take everyday objects and reuse them in an artwork.

2. Once your students have collected their materials, place all objects in a central location and encourage your students to freely explore them. Encourage them to think about how they could use the materials in their own assemblage artwork, using questions such as "What could you make with that?", "How can these items be transformed?", or "What would you like to make with this?" The children can create plans for their proposed artwork by sketching their ideas. Be sure to encourage them to create detailed plans so they know which materials they will need.

Planning phase of assemblage project

3. During the construction phase of this lesson, allow several days for the children to manipulate their objects into their final artworks. The children may wish to paint their objects, so provide adequate drying and storage space in your classroom.

4. Encourage the students to gather only the materials they think they will need and remind them that you are available to hot glue any of the heavier items they have trouble gluing or taping together.

5. Be sure to remind the students to refer to their sketched plans as they work. Once each artwork is completed, encourage each child to give his artwork a title so it can be displayed in the classroom or school.

Documentation:

As this is a longer-term experience, you will have many opportunities to observe and extend children's thinking and experiences if you spend time working alongside them. You can also use the camera to photograph their work during the various project phases. The children's project sketches and final artwork will also serve as documentation of their understanding of object reuse and assemblage art.

Extension Lesson:

This lesson can be extended by repeating the activity with a specific type of object—such as natural materials or man-made objects—and exploring more artwork in these genres of assemblage art.

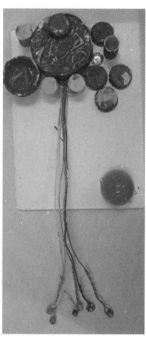

Assemblage art: Balloons made from bottle caps

Painting on Water

Topics:

Earth science: earth materials; visual arts: color, movement, and expression

Objectives:

Children will explore the artworks of artists who paint in the Japanese Suminagashi and the Turkish Ebru styles.

Children will explore the properties of ink painting on water to create their own water paintings.

Materials:

iPad or other tablet

Plastic tub large enough for a 9" x 12" piece of construction paper

Water

White or light-colored construction paper

Liquid inks (will float on top of water)

Liquid watercolors (will dye water) (note: these are not the same as food coloring or traditional watercolor paints)

Acrylic paints (will clump together in water)

Glitter (will float on top of water and stick to paper)

Eyedroppers or pipettes

Creativity Skills:

Exploration

Visualization

Communication/ Collaboration

Flexibility

Originality

Problem solving

Strategic planning

Website to Explore:

Visit the Google Arts and Culture website (https://www.google.com/ culturalinstitute/beta/ search) to explore Suminagashi and Ebru art. The works you locate will emphasize the shared focus on the marbling of colors into distinctive patterns.

Overview:

This lesson will take place over several days in your classroom and connect to your students' understanding of the relationship between water and art making. The creation process will work best if you work with children individually or in pairs so you can direct their attention to working slowly and noticing the changes that take place as they add additional media.

Activity Steps:

1. With your students, spend time looking over images of Suminagashi and Ebru art. Prompt discussion with questions such as "What do you notice about the colors in this artwork?", "How could you describe how the colors are swirled together?", and "Do you see any patterns in this artwork?" You can also talk about how artists paint on all types of surfaces and how these paintings were made by painting on water. Explain to the children how these artists painted on top of water using inks, oils, and paints and then made a print of the painting by placing a piece of paper on top of the water painting—just as the children will do.

2. Fill the plastic tub so that the bottom is completely covered—about one inch of water will work for this process.

3. As you work with each child, invite him to slowly add drops of the available paints and inks with eyedroppers, and direct his attention to how the media move in the water, using questions such as "Does the ink float on the top?", "What happens to the glitter?", and "Can you see any patterns in the colors?"

The process of painting on water

4. Once the child has saturated the surface with color, help him to carefully lay a piece of construction paper on top of the water, taking care not to disturb the surface. Immediately lift off the paper and explore how the painting looks on paper in comparison to on the water.

Documentation:

As this is a longer-term experience, you will have many opportunities to observe and extend children's thinking and experiences if you spend time working alongside them. This is an exploratory activity, so paying careful attention to the children's observations will help you understand their experiences.

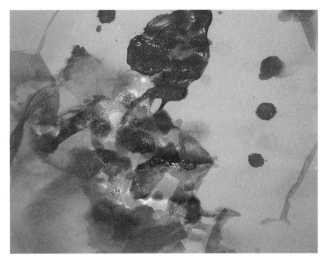

Completed painting on water print

Extension Lesson:

You may want to explore artists who paint on other surfaces and incorporate those experiences into the classroom by inviting your students to paint or draw on other natural materials, such as wood or stone.

Everyday Music

Topics:

Engineering: design and sound; earth science: materials conservation and reuse; musical expression

Objectives:

Children will explore the music of contemporary artists using everyday objects to create sound.

Children will collaborate and create their own sounds using objects in the classroom.

Materials:

iPad or tablet to explore contemporary sound artists and performance artists

Everyday items (spoons, pots, pans, plastic and metal lids, dust brooms, dustpans, plastic cups, and so on. A balance of metal and non-metal items will create unique sound combinations.)

Video-recording device

Creativity Skills:

Exploration

Communication/ Collaboration

Flexibility

Originality

Problem solving

Overview:

This experience can take place in whole groups or in small groups, but it will be loud, so you may want to do it in a larger space or outdoors. You will explore groups that make music using everyday objects—brooms, garbage-can lids, washtubs, kitchenware, and more—to create unique sounds and performances. Two such groups are STOMP and the Electric Junkyard Gamelan. Be sure to preview any videos to ensure that the entire performance meets your standards for child appropriateness.

Activity Steps:

1. Talk with the students about how instruments make sound. What instruments can they name? Which instruments do you have in the classroom? Invite them to think about how artists can make sound with everyday objects like a pan and a spoon.

2. Show the videos you've previewed that feature sound artists and performance artists. Help to direct observations by asking the children to describe the sounds they are hearing as well as the objects the artists are using to create sound.

3. In the materials-gathering phase of the lesson, invite the children to locate materials to use in the creation of sound, or you can preselect items for them to explore.

4. Once every child has an item to use to create sound, encourage them to begin listening to one another's instruments. At first, it will be

Creative Investigations in Early Art

helpful if the children take turns using their objects so that they can experience the different sounds before playing as a whole class.

5. Once everyone has played one object, encourage the children to switch and share objects so that they can experience new sounds.

6. You can record these musical sessions to play back for the children and their families.

Documentation:

Make videos of the children's individual and group sound-making sessions, which can serve as documentation of this exploratory and expressive experience.

Extension Lesson:

This lesson can be extended by creating a semi-permanent outdoor sound wall using everyday objects—this wall can hold pans, pots, muffin tins, and many other objects for children to explore.

Moveable Sculpture

Topics:

Engineering: design; earth science: materials conservation and reuse; visual arts: working in 3-D

Objectives:

Children will explore works of sculpture by contemporary artists in your community.

Children will create their own 3-D, movable sculptures.

Materials:

iPad or other tablet

Large beads and buttons

Creativity Skills:

Exploration

Flexibility

Originality

Problem solving

Strategic planning

Pipe cleaners

Thin 22-gauge (0.64-mm) wire, cut into 12" pieces (1 per child)

Small foam pieces

Website to Explore:

The Public Art Archive website (http://www.publicartarchive.org/) is a database and mobile website of installed public artworks from all over the United States and the world. You can search locally for artwork or contact local art museums or community arts organizations to find out where public art is installed near you.

Overview:

This lesson can be completed in small groups because the children will require some assistance with the manipulation of their wires.

Activity Steps:

1. Before you begin working with the children, bend one end of each wire piece over on itself to prevent any items from falling off the wires as the children string their beads, buttons, or foam pieces.

2. Invite children to share what they know about sculpture. If there is an outdoor sculpture near your school, a walking field trip would be a great way to introduce the children to local art, or you could photograph sculpture in the community that the children may have seen. Encourage them to think about how sculpture can be seen from all sides.

3. Invite the children to look at the materials you've gathered for their sculpture making. You may want to demonstrate how to add materials to the wires.

4. Encourage the children to fill up their wires with beads, buttons, and foam pieces. Once they are finished, you can carefully bend the two ends of a wire together to create a loop for each child.

5. The children can then bend and shape their loops into sculptures that have unique shapes and can rest on a surface.

6. Encourage the children to look at their sculptures from all sides, as they will appear different from different vantage points. You can direct the children's observations by asking them to describe the shapes and colors in their sculptures.

Documentation:

You can create anecdotal notes about the children's understanding of sculpture and their fine-motor abilities as they string materials and manipulate their sculptures.

Extension Lesson:

This lesson can be extended by creating clay sculptures and exploring the work of ceramic artists.

Children's Books

Markel, Michelle. 2012. *The Fantastic Jungles of Henri Rousseau.* Grand Rapids, MI: Eerdmans Books for Young Readers.

The Fantastic Jungles of Henri Rousseau features vibrant, complex images and engaging text to share how Rousseau believed in himself and persevered in his art making, even during times when others did not see his talent.

Rodriguez, Rachel Victoria. 2006. *Through Georgia's Eyes.* New York, NY: Henry Holt and Co.

This book shares the life history of the painter Georgia O'Keefe through a focus on the places that influenced her art. The illustrations show colorful, cut-paper collages that will engage and inspire your students.

Rosenstock, Barb. 2014. *The Noisy Paint Box: The Colors and Sounds of Kandinsky's Abstract Art.* New York, NY: Knopf.

This book will introduce your students to the renowned art of Vasily Kandinsky and provide an engaging story of Kandinsky's childhood art-making beginnings.

Index